My Neighbors

J. Jean Robertson

ROURKE
PUBLISHING

www.rourkepublishing.com

www.rourkepublishing.com

PHOTO CREDITS: Cover: © digitalskillet, © Juan Estey, © Jamie Farrant; Page 3: © flammulated; Page 11: © PacoRomero; Page 15: © InStock; Page 16: © 3000ad; Page 17: © nailzchap; Page 19: © CHRISsadowski, © dem10, © miflippo, © fotovoyager.com

Edited by Meg Greve

Cover design by Renee Brady
Interior design by Tara Raymo

Library of Congress Cataloging-in-Publication Data

Robertson, J. Jean.
  My neighbors / J. Jean Robertson.
    p. cm. -- (Little world social studies)
  Includes bibliographical references and index.
  ISBN 978-1-61590-329-0 (Hard Cover) (alk. paper)
  ISBN 978-1-61590-568-3 (Soft Cover)
  1. United States--Juvenile literature. 2. Canada--Juvenile literature. 3. Mexico--Juvenile literature. I. Title.
  E178.3.R59 2011
  970--dc22

                        2010009263

Rourke Publishing
Printed in the United States of America, North Mankato, Minnesota
033010
033010LP

www.rourkepublishing.com - rourke@rourkepublishing.com
Post Office Box 643328 Vero Beach, Florida 32964

My neighbor is someone who lives
in the next house, town, state,
or **country**.

The United States has two neighbor countries. Let's find them on the **map**.

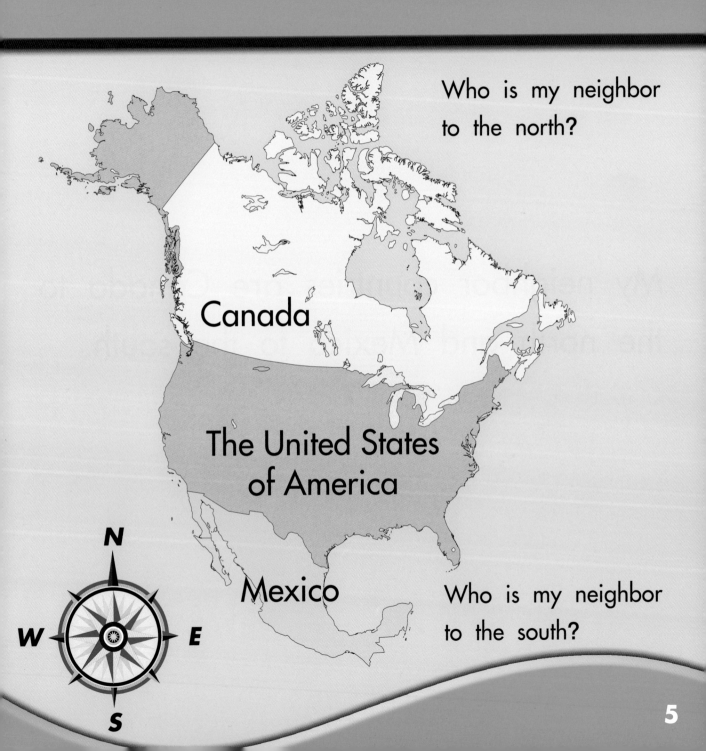

Who is my neighbor to the north?

Canada

The United States of America

Mexico

Who is my neighbor to the south?

N

W E

S

My neighbor countries are Canada to the north and Mexico to the south.

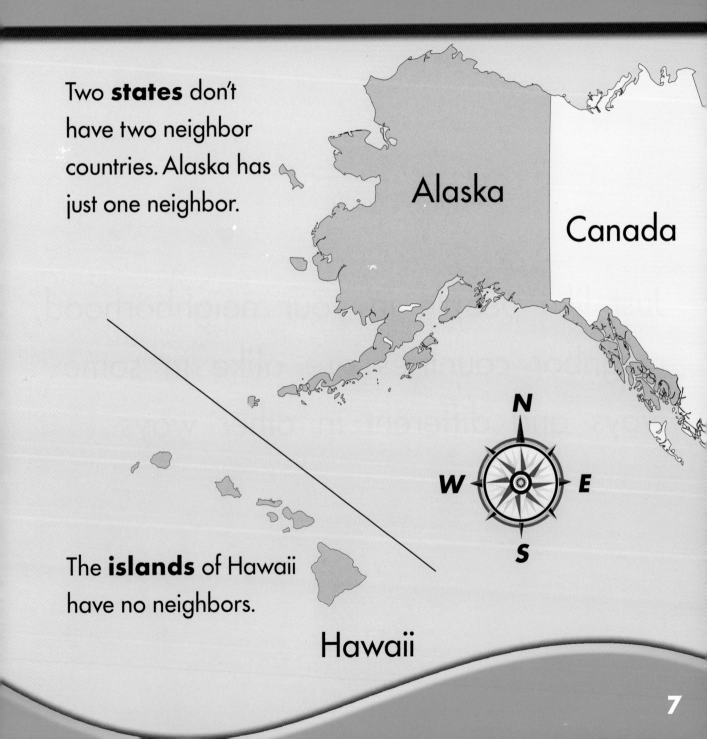

Two **states** don't have two neighbor countries. Alaska has just one neighbor.

Alaska

Canada

The **islands** of Hawaii have no neighbors.

Hawaii

Just like people in your neighborhood, neighbor countries are alike in some ways and different in other ways.

How are we alike?

We all go to school.

We all like playing with our friends.

We all like eating ice cream.

All three countries are divided into smaller areas. The United States has 50 states. Canada has 10 **provinces** and three territories. Mexico has 32 states.

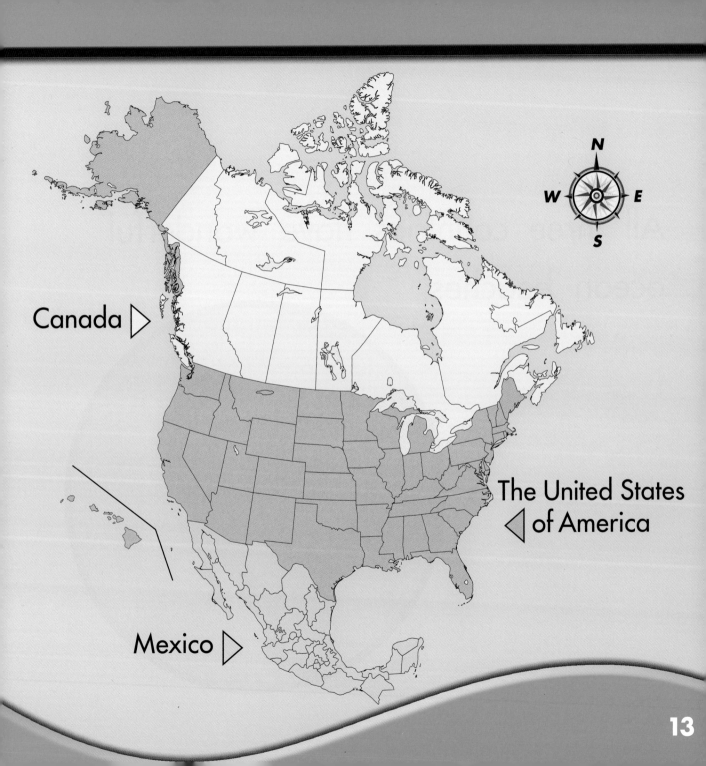

Canada ▷

The United States
◁ of America

Mexico ▷

N
W ⊕ E
S

All three countries have wonderful ocean beaches.

All three countries have tall, beautiful **mountains**.

How are we different?

We speak different languages.

Most Americans speak English.

Many Canadians speak English and French.

Most Mexicans speak Spanish.

Wouldn't it be fun to visit
our neighbors?

Words to know before you go!

	English	French	Spanish
	car	voiture	auto
	hand	main	mano
	shoe	chaussure	zapato
	house	maison	casa

Picture Glossary

country (KUHN-tree): An area of the world that has definite borders and its own government.

islands (EYE-luhnds): Areas of land that are completely surrounded by water.

map (MAP): A drawing showing the shape of an area. Most maps give details about the area, such as towns, mountains, and rivers.

 **mountains** (MOUN-tuhns): Very high parts of the land. The Rocky Mountains stretch across part of Canada and through the United States.

 **provinces** (PROV-uhnssz): Some countries, like Canada, are divided into sections called provinces. Each one has a local government.

 **states** (STATES): Some countries, like the United States and Mexico, are divided into sections called states. Each one has a local government.

Index

Websites

www.kids.nationalgeographic.com/Places/Find/Mexico

www.pocanticohills.org/mexico/mexico.htm

www.kidskonnect.com/subject-index/26-countriesplaces/
304-canada.html

About the Author

J. Jean Robertson, also known as Bushka to her grandchildren and many other kids, loves to read, travel, and write books for children. After teaching for many years, she retired to San Antonio, Florida, where she lives with her husband.